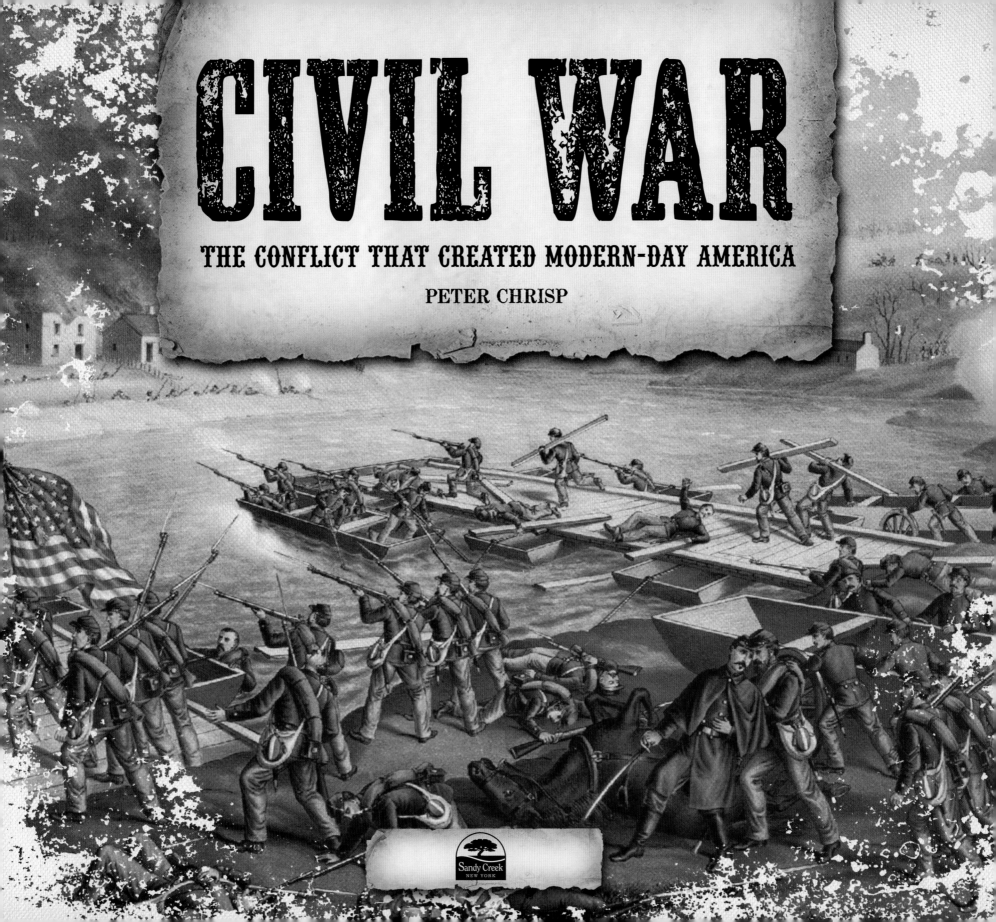

CIVIL WAR

THE CONFLICT THAT CREATED MODERN-DAY AMERICA

PETER CHRISP

Sandy Creek
NEW YORK

UNION

ABRAHAM LINCOLN

ULYSSES S. GRANT

WILLIAM T. SHERMAN

ROBERT ANDERSON

CONFEDERATE

JEFFERSON DAVIS

ROBERT E. LEE

P. G. T. BEAUREGARD

"STONEWALL" JACKSON

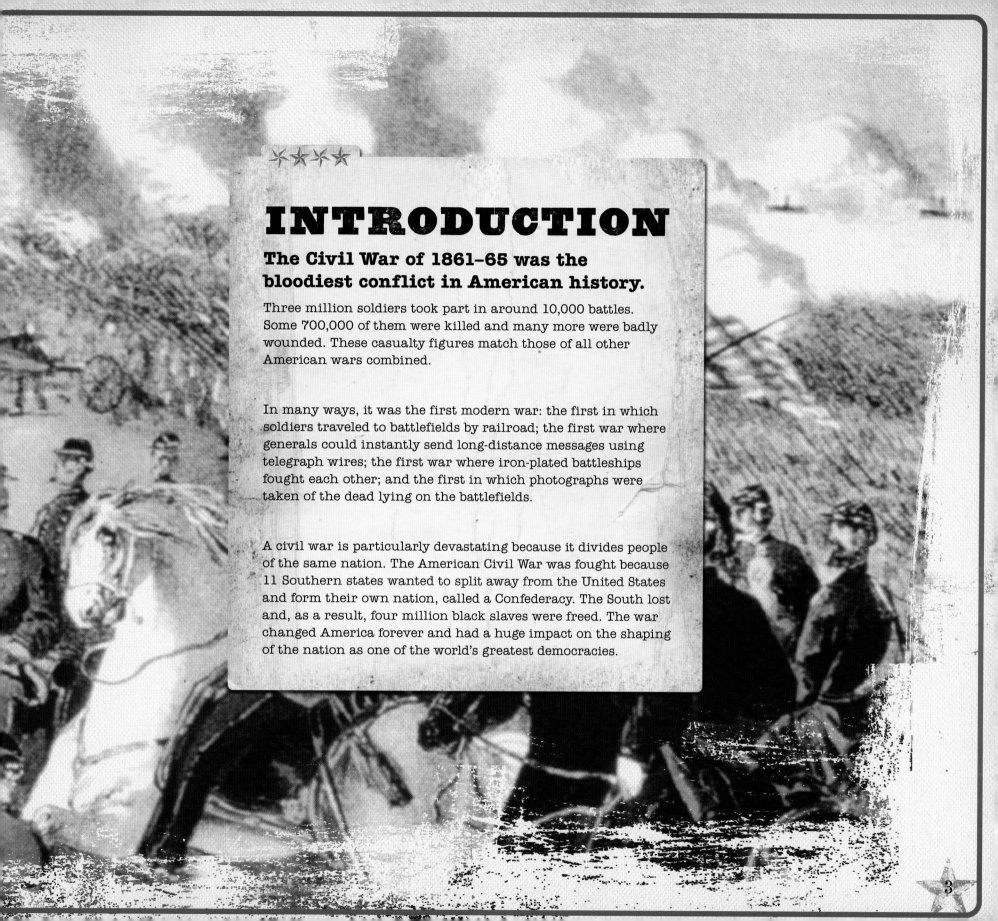

INTRODUCTION

The Civil War of 1861–65 was the bloodiest conflict in American history.

Three million soldiers took part in around 10,000 battles. Some 700,000 of them were killed and many more were badly wounded. These casualty figures match those of all other American wars combined.

In many ways, it was the first modern war: the first in which soldiers traveled to battlefields by railroad; the first war where generals could instantly send long-distance messages using telegraph wires; the first war where iron-plated battleships fought each other; and the first in which photographs were taken of the dead lying on the battlefields.

A civil war is particularly devastating because it divides people of the same nation. The American Civil War was fought because 11 Southern states wanted to split away from the United States and form their own nation, called a Confederacy. The South lost and, as a result, four million black slaves were freed. The war changed America forever and had a huge impact on the shaping of the nation as one of the world's greatest democracies.

NORTH AND SOUTH

In the early nineteenth century, the U.S. was going through great changes. The country was growing, as vast new territories were opened in the West.

Between 1800 and 1850, the U.S. population rose from five million to 23 million people. This was partly due to newcomers arriving from Europe, but mainly because of high birth rates. Many people moved west to settle in new territories that would eventually become states.

THE SLAVERY QUESTION

There were many differences between Northern and Southern states, but the greatest was that the South had 4 million black **slaves**. These people were bought and sold and forced to work for their owners. Slavery was banned in the North. The question was, would the new western territories be slave states or free states where slavery was not allowed?

NORTHERN CITIES

While nine-tenths of Southerners lived in the countryside, three-quarters of Northerners lived in towns and cities. The North saw the rise of new industrial cities like Chicago, whose population grew from just 5,000 in 1840 to 109,000 in 1860.

Construction workers laying railroad track.

RAILROADS

People traveled west on new railroads, which were built across the country. By 1860, there were 30,000 miles of railroad track. The North had a more widespread system of railroads than the South.

TO BE SOLD on board the Ship *Bance-Yland*, on tueſday the 6th of *May* next, at *Aſhley-Ferry*; a choice cargo of about 250 fine healthy

NEGROES,

juſt arrived from the Windward & Rice Coaſt. —The utmoſt care has already been taken, and ſhall be continued, to keep them free from the leaſt danger of being infected with the SMALL-POX, no boat having been on board, and all other communication with people from *Charles-Town* prevented.

Auſtin, Laurens, & Appleby.

N. B. Full one Half of the above Negroes have had the SMALL-POX in their own Country.

★ ★ ★ ★

SLAVES

By the nineteenth century, around 645,000 African men and women had been shipped to North America to work as slaves on plantations, mostly growing tobacco and sugar. Yet there was growing opposition to slavery, which the Northern states had all abolished by 1804. The U.S. government banned the importation of slaves in 1807.

A slave auction in the South at Charleston, South Carolina.

★ ★ ★ ★

STATES' RIGHTS

Every state had its own **legislature**, or law-making assembly. There were arguments over how much power the **federal**, or national, government should hold and how much an individual state should have. The Southerners feared that if the federal government had too much power, it could ban slavery.

Slaves using a cotton gin, which separated the valuable cotton fibers from the seeds.

COTTON

Slavery survived and spread in the South, largely because of Eli Whitney's 1793 invention of the **cotton gin**. This machine meant that, for the first time, it was easy to **mass-produce** cotton. There was a new demand for slaves to pick the cotton, which was shipped to European factories to be made into cloth.

The cotton plant made Southern landowners wealthy.

ABOLITIONISTS

From the early 1800s, an antislavery movement grew in the North. Its members were known as abolitionists.

Abolitionists wanted to put an end to slavery in the states that allowed it. They held public meetings to spread their message and helped runaway slaves to escape to the free states of the North. Southern slave owners feared that abolitionist ideas would lead to an uprising by the slaves.

SOUTHERN ATTITUDES

Many Southerners felt uneasy about slavery, but they worried that freeing the slaves would lead to chaos and bloodshed. Some argued that the slaves working on plantations were better-off than they would be back in Africa, or even as free workers in Northern factories.

A slave family, including children, working in a cotton field in Georgia, 1860.

FREDERICK DOUGLASS

The most famous abolitionist was Frederick Douglass, the son of a slave woman and her white master. After escaping to the North, he wrote his autobiography, describing the suffering of slaves on plantations. It contained many shocking scenes, such as how he had seen his aunt being whipped when he was a child.

Douglass was a powerful public speaker, who spoke to large crowds.

Slaves picking cotton on a Southern plantation.

UNCLE TOM'S CABIN

The suffering of slaves was the subject of Harriet Beecher Stowe's 1852 novel, *Uncle Tom's Cabin*. This was the best-selling novel of the nineteenth century and helped to spread abolitionist ideas among readers in the North.

In *Uncle Tom's Cabin*, the black slave Tom befriends a white girl called Eva.

RUNAWAY SLAVES

Many abolitionists helped runaway slaves escape to freedom using the **"underground railroad."** This was a system of secret routes between the homes of abolitionists, who would shelter the runaways until they reached the North. Slave owners often pursued slaves who had escaped and forced Northern law courts to return them.

Stop the Runaway!

$100 Reward!

Ranaway from the subscriber, living in Clay county, Mo., 3 miles south of Haynesville and 15 miles north of Liberty, a negro boy named SANDY, about 35 years of age, about 5 feet 6 inches high, rather copper color, whiskers in his chin, quick when spoken to, had on when he left brown janes pants and coat, black plush cap, and coarse boots. If apprehended a reward of $25 will be given if taken in Clay county; $50 if out of the county, and $100 if taken out of the State, and delivered to me or confined in jail so that I can get him.

April 3, 1860.   ROBT. THOMPSON.

A newspaper advertisement offering a reward for the capture of an escaped slave.

John Brown and his men, shortly before their capture.

★★★★

JOHN BROWN

In the South, slave owners were often outnumbered by their slaves and they feared a slave rebellion. These fears seemed justified in 1859, when a fanatical abolitionist, John Brown, led a raid on an **armory** full of weapons at Harper's Ferry, Virginia. Brown called on the slaves to rise up, but he was captured and hanged. After his death, John Brown became a hero to abolitionists and was celebrated in songs and poems.

A NATION DIVIDED

The divisions between the North and the South came to a head in November 1860, when Abraham Lincoln was elected President.

Lincoln belonged to the Republican Party, which was against slavery. He was elected with no support from the South, where the Republicans had not campaigned. The election result outraged Southerners. They set about breaking away from the United States, or **Union**, to form their own separate nation, the **Confederacy**.

THE REPUBLICAN PARTY

The Republicans were a new political party, founded in 1854 by antislavery groups in the North. They wanted to stop slavery spreading to the new western territories, which were in the process of becoming states. This would mean that slave states would be greatly outnumbered by free ones. Southerners feared that they would have no power in the national government.

ABRAHAM LINCOLN

Abraham Lincoln was born in 1809 in a one-room log cabin in Kentucky. He was self-educated, teaching himself law before going into politics. As President, his main aim was to save the Union. In 1862, he wrote, "If I could save the Union without freeing any slave I would do it, and if I could save it by freeing all the slaves I would do it."

NATIONAL DIVISIONS

This map shows the divisions between North and South in 1861, and the new western territories. Between the Confederacy and the Union, there were four border states—slave states that did not leave the Union. People here were split between pro- and antislavery groups, and they would provide troops to both sides in the war.

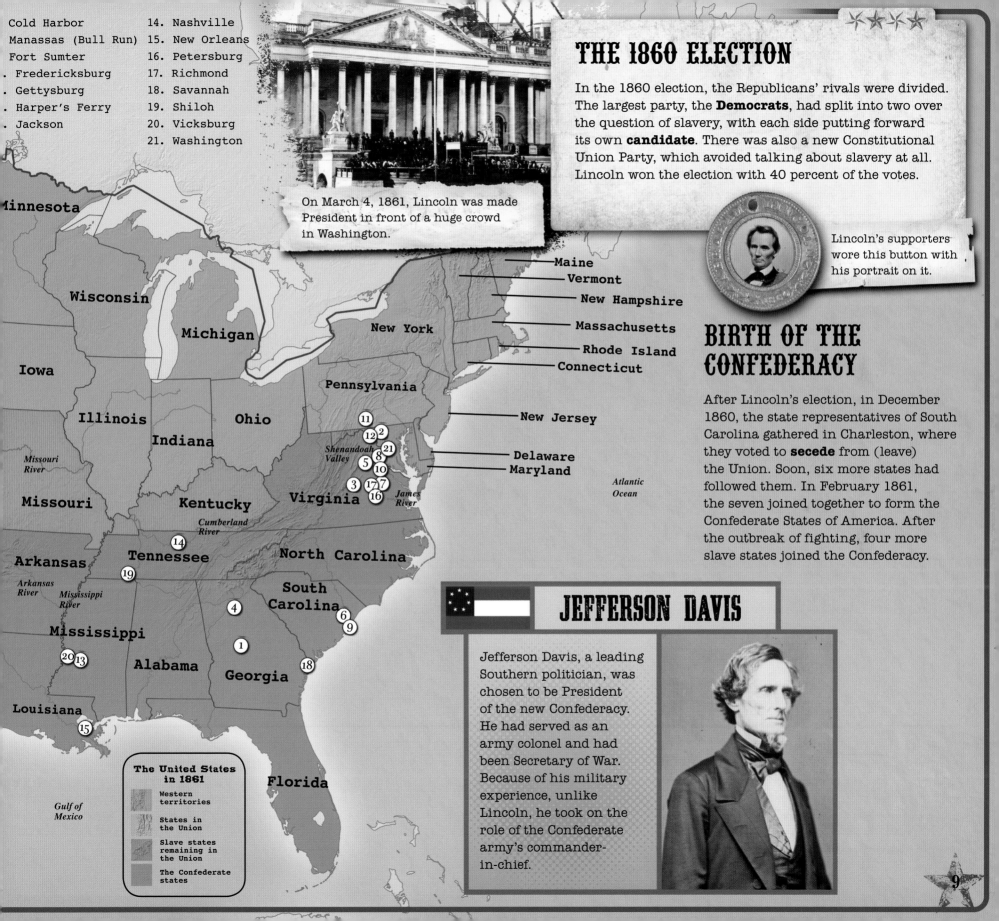

On March 4, 1861, Lincoln was made President in front of a huge crowd in Washington.

THE 1860 ELECTION

In the 1860 election, the Republicans' rivals were divided. The largest party, the **Democrats**, had split into two over the question of slavery, with each side putting forward its own **candidate**. There was also a new Constitutional Union Party, which avoided talking about slavery at all. Lincoln won the election with 40 percent of the votes.

Lincoln's supporters wore this button with his portrait on it.

BIRTH OF THE CONFEDERACY

After Lincoln's election, in December 1860, the state representatives of South Carolina gathered in Charleston, where they voted to **secede** from (leave) the Union. Soon, six more states had followed them. In February 1861, the seven joined together to form the Confederate States of America. After the outbreak of fighting, four more slave states joined the Confederacy.

JEFFERSON DAVIS

Jefferson Davis, a leading Southern politician, was chosen to be President of the new Confederacy. He had served as an army colonel and had been Secretary of War. Because of his military experience, unlike Lincoln, he took on the role of the Confederate army's commander-in-chief.

The United States in 1861

- Western territories
- States in the Union
- Slave states remaining in the Union
- The Confederate states

ATTACK ON FORT SUMTER

The bombardment of Fort Sumter, with the U.S. flag still flying.

In the early hours of April 12, 1861, Confederate guns opened fire on Fort Sumter. These were the first shots fired in the Civil War.

Fort Sumter stood on an island in the middle of Charleston Harbor, South Carolina. It had been built by the U.S. government to defend Charleston against foreign attack. When South Carolina declared that it had left the United States, a small Union force, commanded by Major Robert Anderson, seized the fort to stop it falling into Confederate hands.

RAISING THE STARS AND STRIPES

On the night of December 26, 1861, Major Anderson secretly moved his men into Fort Sumter. They raised the Union flag, the Stars and Stripes. The next morning, the sight of the flag angered the people of Charleston, who had been celebrating their independence from the United States.

A newspaper illustration showing Anderson's men kneeling in prayer as the flag was raised.

A WAITING GAME

The Confederate forces in Charleston were commanded by General P. G. T. Beauregard, who had been Anderson's student in **artillery** science at the West Point Military Academy. For three months, the two sides had waited, unwilling to fire on each other. Beauregard hoped that Anderson would be forced to leave the fort when his supplies ran out.

Beauregard was the first general of the new Confederate army.

BOMBARDMENT

In early April, the Confederates learned that the U.S. government planned to send fresh supplies to the fort. To prevent this, on April 12, Beauregard began to bombard the fort using cannons on the mainland. During the bombardment, the attackers fired 3,340 shots at the fort. These were answered with 1,000 shots from the defenders. Incredibly, nobody was actually seriously injured, but after 34 hours, the exhausted defenders finally surrendered.

This print shows Union artillerymen within the fort returning fire with their cannon.

FIRED FROM FORT MOULTRIE INTO CHARLESTON, S.C. 1861

Despite the heavy cannon fire, there were no casualties.

The Confederate "Stars and Bars" flag flying over Fort Sumter on April 15, 1861.

SURRENDER

After Anderson's surrender, the Confederates took over the fort and raised their own flag, the newly-designed "Stars and Bars." Until the attack on Fort Sumter, it was still possible that war might be avoided. But across the North, there was now outrage at the insult to their flag and fury that U.S. soldiers had been fired upon. The attack on Sumter united Northerners. Southerners were now seen as traitors, and there were calls for revenge.

VOLUNTEERS WANTED!

A recruiting tent in New York with a banner offering cash bounties to volunteers.

At the start of the war, both governments called for thousands of volunteers to join their armies.

There was widespread excitement about joining up. So many men volunteered that it was hard to find guns and uniforms for them. In 1861, young American men had little idea of what warfare would be like. Most had never been away from home before and they saw war as a great adventure. They were also motivated by loyalty to their home state or to the Union. At this time, few on either side felt that they were fighting a war about slavery.

★★★★

CASH BOUNTY

In the North, people who joined the Union army were offered a cash payment called a bounty. For the poor in big cities like New York, this payment made volunteering attractive. But the bounty also resulted in "bounty jumpers": men who would repeatedly join up and run away from each regiment with the bounty money.

A recruitment poster for the Union army.

Forward, Volunteers!
TAKE THE BOUNTIES
WHILE THE OPPORTUNITY LASTS!

$25
19th WARD

$60
KINGS COUNTY

THE DRAFT IS INEVITABLE.
IT CAN'T BE SHIRKED.

ENLIST IN
DURYEA'S
ZOUAVES
SECOND BATTALION
19th WARD
BROOKLYN.

NEW YORK STATE
$50.

UNITED STATES
$100.

CAPTAIN A. T. GROSER.
HEADQUARTERS,
CORNER BEDFORD AVE. AND CLYMER ST.

BAKER & GODWIN, PRINTERS, COR. NASSAU AND SPRUCE STS., NEW YORK.

★★★★

CHOOSING SIDES

Many Americans had to decide which side to fight on. President Lincoln offered Robert E. Lee, a leading general, command of the Union army. Although Lee opposed secession, he felt that his loyalty to his state—Virginia—was greater than his duty to the Union. He resigned from the Union army and joined the Confederacy. Choosing sides was especially difficult in border states, where members of the same family might end up fighting each other.

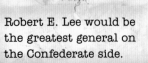

Robert E. Lee would be the greatest general on the Confederate side.

UNIFORMS

At the beginning of the war, there were no standard uniforms. On both sides, soldiers wore blue and gray, which led to men being shot by their own side in the first battles of the war. The most colorful uniforms were those of the Zouaves, who took their name and style from French soldiers in North Africa. Both sides had units of Zouaves.

Confederate troops in dark blue uniforms, just like the Union army.

Many recruits had photographs taken in their new uniforms. These Union Zouaves from New York are wearing short, open-fronted jackets, baggy red pants, and oriental hats.

BOY SOLDIERS

Boys as young as nine joined the army, serving as drummers and messengers. Lincoln said that those under 18 years of age needed their parents' consent to join up, but recruiting officers often ignored this.

Nine-year-old John Clem ran away from home to join the Union army.

FLAGS

The Union already had its own flag, the Stars and Stripes, so the Confederacy needed a new one. The first version, the "Stars and Bars," had horizontal stripes and stars. On both flags, each star stood for a state. As more states joined the Confederacy, more stars were added.

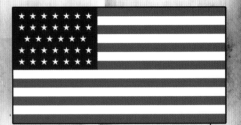

Before the war, the Union flag, the Stars and Stripes, had 33 stars. This Union flag from July 1861 had an extra star for Kansas and still included the Confederate states that had left the Union.

The first Confederate national flag, known as the Stars and Bars, had 13 stars in its final version—one for each of the 11 Confederate states, plus two extra, for Kentucky and Missouri, which the South also claimed.

The Stars and Stripes and the Stars and Bars flags looked similar from a distance, which caused confusion on the battlefield. To solve the problem, the Confederates invented a special battle flag with a distinctive cross design.

THE FIRST BATTLE

General Burnside, on horseback, urging his men to attack Matthews Hill.

At the start of the war, both sides expected the fighting to be over in a few weeks.

Northerners hoped to capture the Confederate capital, Richmond, in Virginia. Southerners believed that a single victory would convince the Northerners to make peace. The first battle of the war took place at Manassas, Virginia, beside the Bull Run River.

In July 1861, General Irvin McDowell set out from Washington at the head of a large army. To get to Richmond, he first had to fight a Confederate army, commanded by General Beauregard, at Manassas, just 25 miles from the Union capital at Washington.

THE UNION ATTACK

McDowell found the Confederate defenders on top of two hills, called Matthews Hill and Henry House Hill. He launched his first attack, led by General Burnside, on Matthews Hill. The Confederates were steadily driven back and began to retreat.

GENERAL McDOWELL

Although McDowell was a senior Union general, he had never commanded troops in battle. He was also worried about his untrained men. President Lincoln reassured him, saying, "You are green, it is true, but they are green also; you are all green alike."

Irvin McDowell, commander of the Union Army of Northeastern Virginia.

STANDING FAST

On top of Henry House Hill, Brigadier Thomas Jackson and his Virginian troops beat off the Union attack. Coming to the support of Jackson, a Confederate general shouted, "Look, there is Jackson standing like a stone wall. Rally behind the Virginians!"

The battle made Jackson a hero and won him the nickname "Stonewall."

REBEL YELL

The Confederates regrouped on Henry House Hill, where Jackson ordered his men to counterattack, saying, "When you charge, yell like furies!" At this, the Confederates swept down on the Union forces with screaming battle cries. Union soldiers called this terrifying sound, which would be heard on many more Civil War battlefields, the "rebel yell."

"We have whipped them! They ran like sheep. Give me 5,000 fresh men and I will be in Washington City tomorrow!"

Stonewall Jackson to Jefferson Davis following the battle.

This painting shows Virginian cavalrymen attacking the Union infantry at Manassas.

Union soldiers and civilian spectators fleeing from the battlefield.

★★★★ RETREAT!

The Union forces broke and ran for their lives. They were joined in their retreat by many civilians, who had come in carriages to watch the battle. Luckily for the Union soldiers, the Confederates were too disorganized to follow them.

The battle, called First Bull Run in the North and First Manassas in the South, showed that the war would not be won quickly. Yet it convinced many Southerners that they could win the war.

FIRST BULL RUN: BATTLE STATISTICS

UNION		CONFEDERATES
Soldiers 18,000	★	Soldiers 18,000
Killed 460	★	Killed 387
Wounded 1,124	★	Wounded 1,582
Missing or captured 1,312	★	Missing or captured 13

A SOLDIER'S LIFE

Union soldiers in front of their Sibley tent, which could hold up to 12 soldiers.

After joining up, the new recruits had to adjust to the hard realities of daily life as a soldier.

They lived together in crowded camps, usually in canvas tents. In the winter, when it was too cold to live in tents, they cut down trees and built log cabins. The soldiers lived on a boring diet of hard, dry bread, dried or salted pork, dried vegetables, and coffee. At night, they slept on the ground, wrapped in blankets that they carried in their **haversacks**.

A Confederate log cabin camp at Manassas in the winter of 1861–2.

✯✯✯✯ CAMPING OUT

At the start of the war, most of the Union army lived in large, conical tents, called Sibley tents. From 1862, these were replaced by smaller tents which were easier to carry. Each soldier had a rectangle of cloth that could be joined to another man's piece to make a two-man tent called a dog or pup tent.

Soldiers would gather around their campfires to eat and keep warm.

✯✯✯✯ FOOD

Groups of six to eight men ate together, taking turns to cook over an open fire, usually in a metal skillet. Their dried bread, called hardtack, had to be ground up and recooked. It could be fried with dried vegetables and meat or soldiers made it into a dough which they wrapped around their bayonets and cooked over the fire. Problems with food supplies meant that soldiers often had to eat whatever they could find by **foraging**.

COFFEE

Soldiers loved drinking coffee and would also chew coffee beans while marching. Because of the Union **blockade**, coffee was in short supply in the South. Confederate soldiers often had to drink fake coffee made from roasted acorns and chicory.

An 1862 coffee label showing Union soldiers and flags.

On a march, each soldier carried his own supply of drinking water in a canteen.

★★★★
CAMP LIFE

Life in camp could be boring, with long periods of **drill** (training) and chores such as collecting firewood or clean water. Soldiers on both sides kept up their spirits by singing hymns and songs. Many patriotic and sentimental songs were specially composed for the soldiers during the war and each side had its own favorites.

Hardtack was made in vast quantities for the soldiers of both sides.

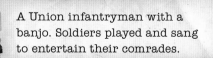

A Union infantryman with a banjo. Soldiers played and sang to entertain their comrades.

"We're tenting tonight on the old camp ground. Give us a song to cheer our weary hearts: a song of home and friends we love so dear."

Lyrics from *Tenting Tonight*, a song popular with Union soldiers.

UNION SOLDIERS

About half of the Union soldiers were farmers. The rest were mostly laborers and tradesmen from Northern towns and cities.

These ordinary civilians had to be turned into soldiers, ready to shoot and to withstand enemy fire on a battlefield. A quarter of Union soldiers were born overseas. They had emigrated to the U.S. in search of a better life, only to find themselves fighting in a civil war.

A first lieutenant of the Union cavalry with his standard-issue saber.

UNION CAVALRY

The role of the Union cavalry was to scout, to raid enemy territory, or to pursue fleeing enemies following a battle. Cavalrymen were armed with sabers, for fighting on horseback, and short rifles called carbines—they would usually dismount to fire these.

When they joined the army, soldiers often posed for photographs with their own revolvers.

RIFLE DRILL

Civilians were made into soldiers through **rifle** drill—memorizing the actions needed to fire a rifle by doing them over and over again. On the battlefield, they would be able to rapidly load and fire their weapons without stopping to think.

"The first thing in the morning is drill, then drill, then drill again."
Union Private Oliver Norton

SPRINGFIELD RIFLE

Springfield rifles were made in the North, in Springfield, Massachusetts, but both sides used them.

The most widely used Union weapon was the Springfield rifle, a single-shot weapon that could be deadly, even at long range. A trained soldier could fire three times a minute and hit an enemy 500 yards away.

INFANTRYMEN

Union infantrymen were better dressed and equipped than Confederate soldiers. In fact, soldiers often felt that they had too much equipment. To lighten their load on the march, they would often discard items such as their heavy winter overcoats.

A soldier's cartridge pouch held lead bullets and paper cartridges filled with gunpowder.

Every soldier carried his own mess cutlery—a knife, fork, and spoon—in his **haversack**.

Forage cap

Infantrymen wore blue forage caps, which were also called kepis.

Knapsack

On his back the soldier carried a black cotton **knapsack** holding his piece of tent cloth, spare clothes, wash kit, and a sewing kit called a "housewife." His rubber-coated waterproof blanket was rolled up on top.

Cap pouch

This pouch held metal percussion caps filled with explosive that were used to fire bullets from a rifle.

Springfield rifle

Infantrymen used rifles for accurate shooting. They fired lead bullets called Minié balls.

Bayonet

A bayonet 18 inches long could be fixed to the end of the rifle to make a deadly stabbing weapon.

Uniform jacket

A dark blue coat with four buttons was the most common style of Union infantry jacket.

Haversack

The haversack, worn on the soldier's left side, held food rations such as coffee beans and hardtack. On top, he carried his water canteen.

Boots and gaiters

Union soldiers were better supplied with boots than Confederate soldiers. Leather gaiters kept water and dirt out in muddy conditions.

CONFEDERATE SOLDIERS

Unlike the Northerners, who they called Yankees, most Confederate soldiers were from the countryside.

Usually, they were small-scale farmers and too poor to own their own slaves. The Yankee nickname for a Confederate was "Johnny Reb" (from "rebel").

This young Confederate in a homemade uniform looks more like a farmer than a soldier.

RAGGED SOLDIERS

There was a shortage of soap in the South, so the men had trouble washing themselves and their clothes. They might wear the same filthy clothes for months, until they rotted away. The biggest problem was a lack of shoes, as the soles wore out during long marches. Soldiers sometimes had to go barefoot.

"It is not safe to pull off shoes and go to sleep or one would wake up minus a pair."
Lieutenant R. McGill, letter to his wife, July 30, 1864.

HOMEMADE UNIFORMS

The official Confederate uniform combined a gray woolen jacket with sky blue or gray pants. However, as uniforms were in short supply in the South, many Confederate soldiers wore a homemade version.

This jacket, worn by Captain John Bullock of the Confederate cavalry, shows the official gray uniform of the South.

ENFIELD RIFLE

At the beginning of the war, the Confederate government bought thousands of British-made Enfield rifles. Confederates also used Union Springfield rifles, captured in battle. The two rifles were so similar that they could fire the same bullets.

CAVALRYMEN

The South's leading cavalry general, Nathan Bedford Forrest, raised his own cavalry force at the start of the war. Confederates were usually better horsemen than Northerners. In the South, where roads were poor, it was common to ride on horseback. Many Southerners brought their own horses with them when they joined the cavalry.

INFANTRYMEN

The Confederate infantryman was armed much like a Union soldier, with a similar rifle and ammunition. However, he would generally have less equipment and his clothes would often be ragged and dirty.

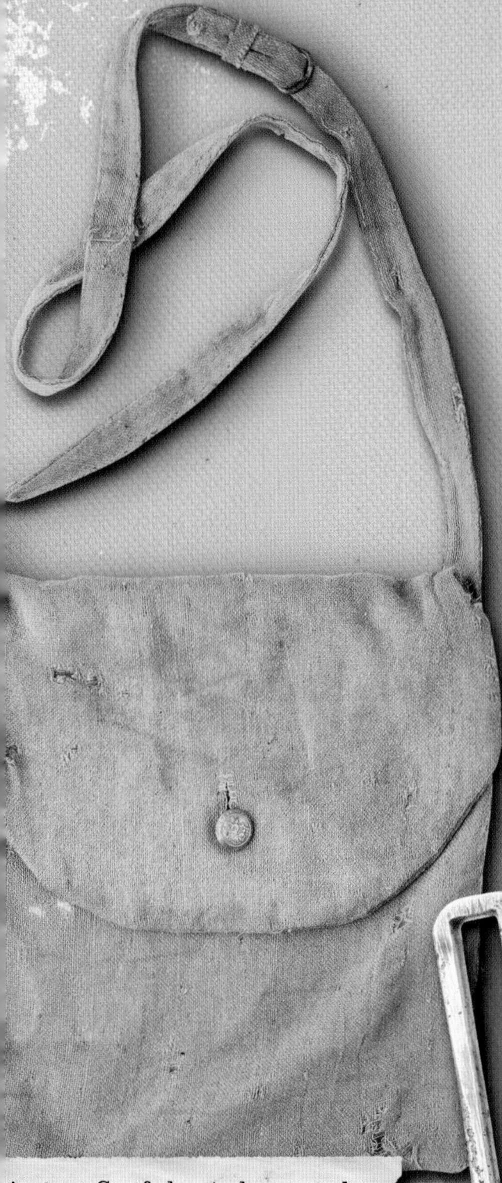

Uniform jacket

Confederate infantrymen wore long gray overcoats, or shorter waist-length jackets like the one shown here. They were meant to be gray, but some were dyed a butternut color.

Hat

This soldier wears the official Confederate peaked forage cap, but many wore broad-brimmed slouch hats that gave greater protection from the sun.

Enfield rifle

This infantryman carries a British-made Enfield rifle and bayonet.

Knapsack

An infantryman's black leather knapsack held all his cooking and eating kit, plus spare gunpowder and ammunition. The soldier's bedroll could be strapped on top.

Cartridge box

This pouch held bullets and gunpowder cartridges. It was made of waterproof leather to keep them dry.

Canteen

This soldier has a water canteen made of tin, but some were made of wood.

Shoes

This Confederate is lucky to have shoes. They may have been taken from a dead Northern soldier.

This gray Confederate haversack held a soldier's food rations.

The "CS" on this metal belt buckle stands for "Confederate Service."

CAMPAIGNS OF 1862

Union troops fought off the Confederate attack at Shiloh alongside a track called the "hornet's nest."

As the war entered its second year, it became clear that it would not be over quickly.

There were two big Union campaigns in early 1862. In the east, General George McClellan launched a seaborne invasion of the Virginia Peninsula in a new attempt to capture the Confederate capital, Richmond. Meanwhile, in the west, General Ulysses S. Grant invaded Tennessee.

★ ★ ★ ★

THE BATTLE OF SHILOH

On April 6, Grant's army came under surprise attack in the woods at Shiloh. Suffering terrible casualties, the Union troops held on until evening, when reinforcements arrived. When one of his officers suggested retreating, Grant said, "No, sir, I propose to attack at daylight and **whip** them." The next day, the Union troops attacked and won. After the Battle of Shiloh, which left 20,000 casualties, people realized that the war would be long and bloody.

ULYSSES S. GRANT

Following the terrible losses at Shiloh, Northern politicians called on Lincoln to remove General Ulysses S. Grant from command. The President refused, saying, "I need this man. He fights."

PENINSULA CAMPAIGN

In March 1862, McClellan invaded the Virginia Peninsula with an army of 100,000 men. An overcautious general, McClellan achieved little. In late June, he was driven back by the Confederate General Robert E. Lee in a series of battles, and McClellan's peninsula campaign was abandoned.

Union troops, including artillerymen, in their camp on the Virginia Peninsula.

SHILOH: BATTLE STATISTICS

UNION	CONFEDERATES
66,812 troops	44,699 troops
1,754 killed	1,728 killed
8,408 wounded	8,012 wounded
2,885 captured/ missing	959 captured/ missing

SHENANDOAH VALLEY

From March to June 1862, the Confederate general Stonewall Jackson, with just 17,000 men, won victories against three larger Union armies in the Shenandoah Valley, western Virginia. His men marched rapidly over great distances to launch surprise attacks. Jackson's **campaign** stopped these Union armies from being sent to reinforce McClellan.

Union cavalrymen cross the Shenandoah River in pursuit of Jackson's army.

STONEWALL JACKSON

A deeply religious man, Stonewall Jackson was completely fearless in battle. He said, "My religious belief teaches me to feel as safe in battle as in bed. God has fixed the time for my death."

Jackson's valley campaign made him a hero in the South.

CONSCRIPTION

Realizing that the war would be a long one, each side introduced conscription (forced service) in the army. In the North, however, you could pay someone to take your place. In the South, slave-owners with a lot of slaves were excused. As a result, the conflict came to be seen by many as a "rich man's war, a poor man's fight."

Vol. 35.
O. 493.

Olivia Ditson & Co.
Proprietor
Sept. 29 18

Wanted
A
SUBSTITUTE.

"Always mystify, mislead, and surprise the enemy if possible." General Stonewall Jackson

This Northern anticonscription cartoon shows a poor man saying "I'm drafted" while a richer man says "I ain't."

NAVAL WARFARE

The Civil War was also fought at sea and on the great rivers of the South.

The North, with a much bigger navy, blockaded the ports of the South to stop the supply of weapons and raw materials to the Confederacy. Both sides built new, **ironclad**, steam-powered battleships to fight this naval war.

BLOCKADE!

To blockade the South, Union ships had to patrol 3,000 miles of Southern coastline. At the beginning of the war, Confederates could get through using blockade runners: small, fast ships that sailed at night. Yet the blockade became increasingly effective. By the end of the war, the Union navy had captured 1,149 Confederate vessels and had sunk 350 more.

THE IRONCLADS CLASH

In March 1862, the first Confederate ironclad, CSS *Virginia*, steamed into the James River, where she sank one Union warship and crippled another. The Union Navy sent the USS *Monitor* to counterattack. *Monitor* was the North's first ironclad and had a revolving gun turret. The two ships bombarded each other for two hours, but neither was damaged and the battle ended without a clear winner.

The ironclads *Monitor* (left) and *Virginia* (right).

The crew of the USS *Monitor* on the iron deck of their ship.

24

HIDDEN DANGERS

The Confederates defended their coasts with exploding mines, called **torpedoes**, suspended beneath the water by floating barrels. During the war, 58 ships were sunk by torpedoes. Northerners thought these hidden weapons were cowardly.

A Union drawing of a Confederate torpedo found in the Potomac River.

ADMIRAL FARRAGUT

The most famous naval commander of the war was the Union's Admiral David Farragut. On August 5, 1864, he won a great battle over the Confederate navy in Mobile Bay, Alabama, after taking his fleet through waters that were full of torpedoes.

David Farragut was the first admiral in U.S. naval history.

"Damn the torpedoes! Full steam ahead!"

U.S. Admiral David Farragut, at the Battle of Mobile Bay, 1864.

The night battle off New Orleans. Farragut's **flagship** is in the center.

THE CAPTURE OF NEW ORLEANS

Farragut's greatest victory was the capture of New Orleans, the South's largest city, on April 28, 1862. To reach the city, Farragut had to fight his way past two powerful forts. After bombarding them for five days, Farragut's ships sailed past and up the Mississippi. Then, following a night battle with the Confederate river fleet, Farragut captured New Orleans.

FIGHTING FOR FREEDOM

In 1862, Lincoln decided to free, or emancipate, all the slaves in the Confederate states.

He knew that this would weaken the South, which needed slave labor. But it was a risky act, as many Northeners opposed making the war about slavery as much as reuniting the country. Lincoln needed a big victory to ensure support in the North before he could declare **emancipation**. He finally got his victory at Antietam.

THE BATTLE OF ANTIETAM

In September 1862, a Confederate army led by Robert E. Lee invaded Maryland. On September 17, it clashed with General McClellan's much larger Union army at Antietam. Neither side won the battle, but Lee retreated from Maryland and Lincoln was able to claim it as a Union victory.

THE HORROR OF WAR

The Battle of Antietam was the bloodiest in American history, with 23,000 casualties. In October 1862, the Union photographer Matthew Brady exhibited photos of the dead at Antietam. It was the first time that the public had seen the human cost of the war.

Confederate dead on the battlefield of Antietam.

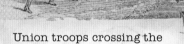
Union troops crossing the bridge over Antietam creek.

ANTIETAM: BATTLE STATISTICS

UNION	CONFEDERATES
Soldiers 75,000	Soldiers 40,000
Killed 2,108	Killed 1,546
Wounded 9,549	Wounded 7,752
Missing or captured 753	Missing or captured 1,018

LINCOLN'S VISIT

In October, President Lincoln visited Antietam and was shown the battlefield. Lincoln was frustrated that McClellan had not pursued Lee's army. When they had their photograph taken together, Lincoln joked that McClellan would have no trouble standing still!

President Lincoln with General McClellan after the Battle of Antietam.

FREEING THE SLAVES

Lincoln's Emancipation Proclamation said that all the slaves in **rebel** states were free. It meant that the war was no longer about preserving the past, but about creating a better future. Emancipation ended Confederate hopes of getting help from nations who were against slavery, such as Britain or France. It also undermined the Confederate war effort, as "freed" slaves ran away to join the Union.

A print of Lincoln's Emancipation Proclamation of January 1, 1863.

"Now I go in for a war of emancipation and I am ready and willing to do my share of the work."

Union Sergeant Eli Pickett, letter to his wife, March 1863.

AFRICAN AMERICAN SOLDIERS AT WAR

From 1863, black men were able to join the Union army, serving in special regiments called the USCT (United States Colored Troops). Around 180,000 men joined up. They were paid less than whites and could not become officers, yet they fought bravely. The Confederates hated black soldiers and often killed them if they captured them.

Like their white comrades, African American soldiers proudly posed for photographs.

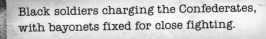

Black soldiers charging the Confederates, with bayonets fixed for close fighting.

CASUALTIES AND PRISONERS

Although the weapons and tactics of the Civil War made it the first modern war, medical treatment was still primitive.

Surgeons operating on the wounded often used dirty instruments. For every soldier killed in battle, two more died of disease. Civil War rifles caused terrible, bone-shattering injuries. Those wounded in the chest or head often died. The usual treatment for wounds to the arms or legs was **amputation**: cutting off the injured limb.

Army doctors giving first aid to the wounded on the battlefield.

HELPING THE WOUNDED

On the battlefield, the doctors had to quickly decide if wounded soldiers were likely to live or die. Those with a chance of survival were carried on stretchers to a horse-drawn ambulance. They were taken to a field hospital, often in a tent, where surgeons would be waiting.

★★★★★ FIELD SURGERY

In a field hospital, a patient was given chloroform to dull his pain before a surgeon operated on his wound. Surgeons at that time did not understand that germs spread diseases. Due to a shortage of water, they might use the same instruments for days without washing them. As a result, many wounded soldiers died of infections.

Wounded Union soldiers being loaded onto an ambulance.

No. 41,258
J. Reichenbach.
Artificial Leg
Patented Jany. 12th 1864.

Making artificial limbs for amputees was a major industry following the war.

A drawing of surgeons opera on a patient at the field hosp at Chancellorsville.

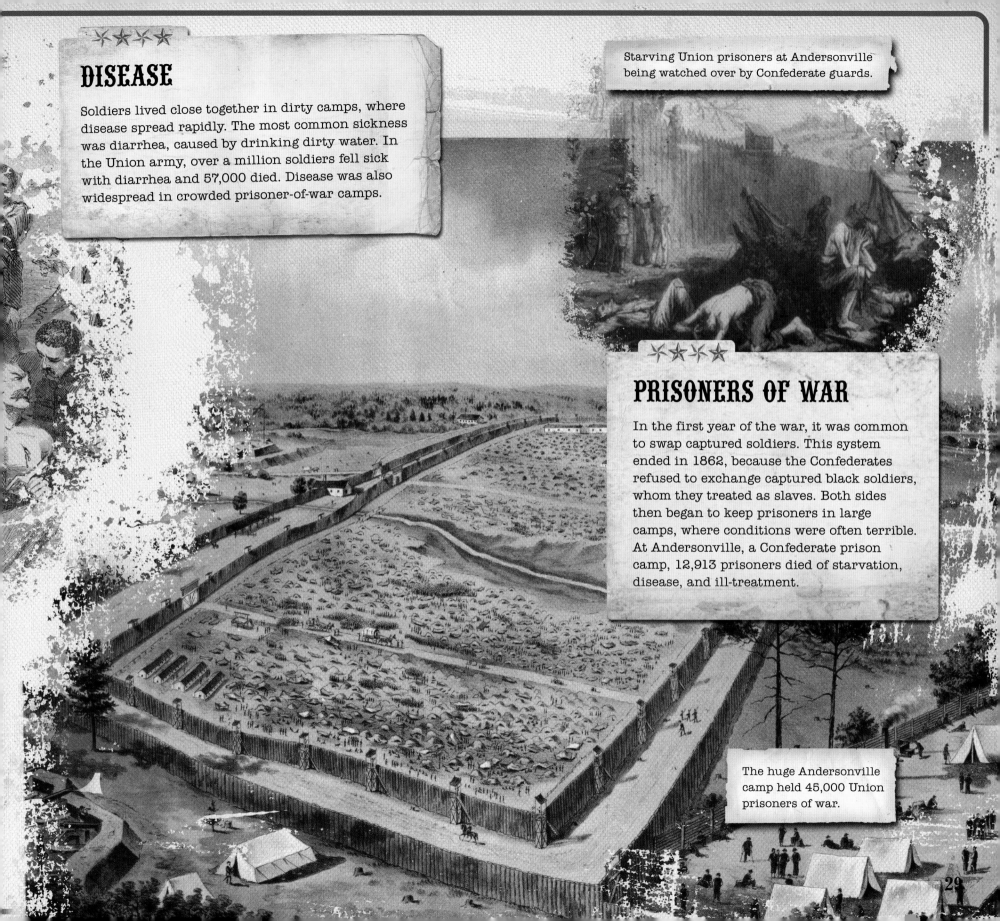

DISEASE

Soldiers lived close together in dirty camps, where disease spread rapidly. The most common sickness was diarrhea, caused by drinking dirty water. In the Union army, over a million soldiers fell sick with diarrhea and 57,000 died. Disease was also widespread in crowded prisoner-of-war camps.

Starving Union prisoners at Andersonville being watched over by Confederate guards.

PRISONERS OF WAR

In the first year of the war, it was common to swap captured soldiers. This system ended in 1862, because the Confederates refused to exchange captured black soldiers, whom they treated as slaves. Both sides then began to keep prisoners in large camps, where conditions were often terrible. At Andersonville, a Confederate prison camp, 12,913 prisoners died of starvation, disease, and ill-treatment.

The huge Andersonville camp held 45,000 Union prisoners of war.

29

LEE'S VICTORIES

Robert E. Lee, commander of the Confederate Army of Northern Virginia, became the most famous general of the Civil War. In a series of battles, he defeated one Union general after another.

Lee was a great risk taker and always willing to attack, unlike most of the Union generals whom he fought against. He was always confident in his ability to win battles and believed that his men could defeat any Union army.

The Battle of Fredericksburg in Virginia

ROBERT E. LEE

Lee was tall and imposing and looked like a heroic general should. He was praised as a great general— not just in the South, but also in Northern newspapers.

"General Lee knows his business and the army has yet known no such word as fail."

Charleston Mercury newspaper, December 1862

THE BATTLE OF FREDERICKSBURG

In December 1862, the Union general Ambrose Burnside launched an attack on Lee's army at Fredericksburg, Virginia. The Confederates were in a well-defended position on higher ground and the battle was a disastrous defeat for Burnside, who lost more than twice as many men as Lee.

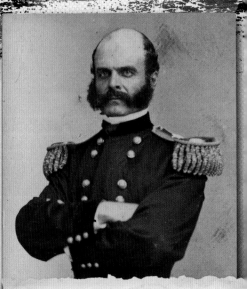

General Burnside, commander of the Union Army of the Potomac.

LEE'S SURPRISE ATTACK

Lee came up with a daring plan to defeat Hooker's larger army. He sent most of his men, under Stonewall Jackson, on a 12-mile march around the Union army to make a surprise attack from the rear. Lee remained facing the Union lines with a small force. The plan worked: when Jackson's troops attacked the Union soldiers, they fled in panic.

General Hooker was nicknamed "Fighting Joe" by the Northern newspapers.

JOE HOOKER

Following the terrible defeat at Fredericksburg, General Joe Hooker replaced Burnside as commander of the Army of the Potomac. In May 1863, he led his men to Chancellorsville in Virginia to face Lee's army. With twice as many men as the Confederates, Hooker said, "I have got Lee just where I want him."

Union troops flee following the surprise attack.

JACKSON WOUNDED

After the battle, Jackson was riding back in the dark when he was accidentally shot by his own **pickets**. Jackson had to have his left arm amputated. Hearing the news, Lee said, "Jackson has lost his left arm, but I have lost my right." A week later, Stonewall Jackson died of pneumonia.

Stonewall Jackson was hit by three bullets: two in the left arm and one in the right hand.

CIVILIANS

The outcome of the Civil War depended as much on civilians, far from the battlefield, as on the soldiers at the front.

Civilians grew food to feed the armies or worked in factories making weapons, uniforms, and ammunition. On each side, there were also spies, secretly passing on information about military plans and troop movements.

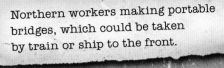
Northern workers making portable bridges, which could be taken by train or ship to the front.

★★★★ WAR INDUSTRY

The North began the war with thousands more factories than the South. Unlike Southern factories, these were far from battlefields and safe from enemy attack. The war years saw a huge growth in certain Northern industries, especially those producing firearms, gunpowder, and shoes.

★★★★ WOMEN AT WAR

Women played an important role in the war. They nursed the wounded and made uniforms and bandages. Wives kept farms going while their husbands were away at the front. At least 250 women also joined the armies as soldiers, disguising themselves as men. Some of the most important spies were women.

These women are filling rifle cartridges with gunpowder.

ROSE O'NEAL GREENHOW

The most famous Confederate spy was Rose O'Neal Greenhow, a Washington society hostess who passed information about Union plans to the Confederates. After being caught and imprisoned, she defiantly flew the Confederate flag from her cell window.

THE WILL TO FIGHT

Both governments worried about civilian morale, meaning the will of the people to continue the war. This was a particular problem for Lincoln, who had to win an election in 1864, while the country was still at war. Lincoln was often criticized in Northern newspapers. In the South, most newspapers supported the Confederate government.

This 1864 cartoon shows Lincoln having a nightmare in which he loses that year's election.

Soldiers opening fire on the New York rioters.

DRAFT RIOTS

The introduction of **conscription** led to riots in New York in July 1863. Irish New Yorkers didn't like being forced to fight a war to free slaves, so they attacked blacks and their property. Up to 120 civilians were killed and around 2,000 were injured.

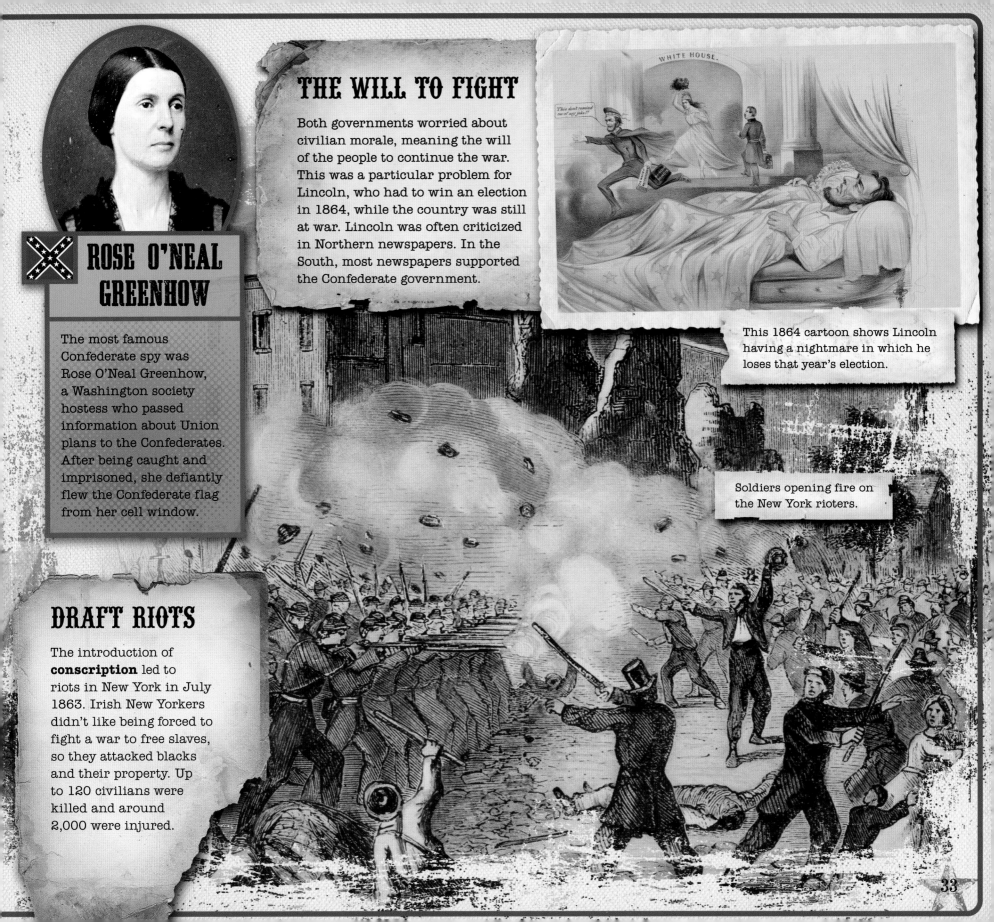

GETTYSBURG

UNION	CONFEDERATES
Soldiers 93,921	Soldiers 71,699
Killed 3,512	Killed 4,708
Wounded 14,531	Wounded 12,693
Missing or captured 5,369	Missing or captured 5,830

Lee's great victory at Chancellorsville encouraged him to invade the North again in the summer of 1863. The result would be a three-day battle at Gettysburg—the largest battle ever fought in the U.S.

On July 1, 1863, Lee led his army of 71,699 men to Gettysburg, hoping to find supplies in the area, especially shoes, which Lee's men desperately needed. Also heading for Gettysburg was the Union general George Meade, with almost 94,000 men.

GENERAL MEADE

Meade, the best general Lee had faced, set up a strong defensive position and awaited the Confederate attack. Lee was advised not to attack, but he said, "They are there in position and I am going to whip them or they are going to whip me."

PICKETT'S CHARGE

After two days of fighting, the Battle of Gettysburg ended when Lee ordered General George Pickett's division to charge into the center of Meade's army. The attack was a disaster and the division was almost wiped out. Returning, Pickett wept as he told Lee, "I have no division now." Lee replied, "Your men have done all that men can do. The fault is certainly my own." Defeated, Lee retreated south.

Pickett sending his division of 12,500 men to attack the Union lines.

THE GETTYSBURG ADDRESS

To honor the dead Union soldiers, a new cemetery was built on the battlefield. On November 19, 1863 at the dedication ceremony, Abraham Lincoln made a speech in which he explained why the war was being fought. Although he spoke for just two minutes, Lincoln's speech, known as the Gettysburg Address, would become the most famous ever given by a U.S. President.

UNKNOWN SOLDIERS

A total of 8,220 dead soldiers were hastily buried after the battle. The Union dead were later reburied, with gravestones giving their names. However, 979 of them could not be identified.

UNKNOWN
U.S. SOLDIER

"We here highly resolve that these dead shall not have died in vain—that this nation, under God, shall have a new birth of freedom—and that government of the people, by the people, for the people, shall not perish from the Earth."

Abraham Lincoln, Gettysburg Address, November 19, 1863

VICKSBURG

Just a day after the Battle of Gettysburg, General Grant won a second great victory for the North.

On July 4, 1863, following a brilliant military campaign, General Ulysses S. Grant captured Vicksburg in Mississippi. Vicksburg was the last Confederate stronghold on the Mississippi River. Its capture gave the North complete control over the great river and split the Confederacy in two.

★ ★ ★ ★

BRAVING THE GUNS

To take Vicksburg, Grant had to lead his army deep into enemy territory. He began by sending a fleet of gunboats down the Mississippi at night, past the Confederate gunners in Vicksburg. Although the Confederates scored 68 hits, only one Union gunboat was sunk.

Grant's army then marched down the west bank of the Mississippi to a point below Vicksburg, where the soldiers met gunboats that ferried them across the river. Cut off from their own supply lines, the Union soldiers had to live off the enemy's land.

Union gunboats running past Vicksburg under fire from the Confederates' artillery.

TAKING VICKSBURG

Before taking Vicksburg, Grant had to deal with the army of General Joseph E. Johnston, to the east, at the Mississippi state capital, Jackson. On May 14, 1863, Grant's deputies, Sherman and McPherson, defeated Johnston's army and captured the city. Grant could now cut off all supplies to Vicksburg.

Grant laid siege to Vicksburg for five weeks. As well as shelling the city, his men tunneled under its walls and planted mines. The Confederate defenders ran short of supplies and were forced to eat their own mules, as well as rats.

Grant's army was helped by the Union navy, which shelled the Confederates' positions.

SURRENDER

Without hope of relief and on the verge of starvation, the Confederates finally surrendered at Vicksburg on July 4, 1863. Grant met the Confederate commander, General Pemberton, to discuss the terms of surrender and later wrote, "The fall of the Confederacy was settled when Vicksburg fell."

General Grant (left) and General Pemberton (right).

This monument was set up to mark the spot where Grant and Pemberton agreed to the surrender.

INVADING THE SOUTH

In March 1864, Lincoln made Ulysses S. Grant head of the Union armies. Grant had a plan to end the war.

While Grant traveled east to fight Robert E. Lee in Virginia, he sent General Sherman to invade Georgia. Sherman promised a campaign of destruction that would "make Georgia howl."

ULYSSES S. GRANT

★★★★ GRANT AGAINST LEE

For the first time, the two greatest Civil War generals were fighting each other. For 11 months, from May 1864, their armies fought daily battles with terrible losses on each side. Grant was an aggressive and ruthless general and seized every opportunity to attack Lee's army, no matter how many casualties he suffered.

TRENCH WARFARE

In June 1864, Grant tried to capture the Confederates' railroad junction at Petersburg, about 20 miles south of Richmond, Virginia. To defend Petersburg, Lee's army dug many miles of trenches. Lee's aim was simply to hold out, while causing as many Union casualties as possible. Nine months of trench warfare followed.

A dead Confederate soldier lying in one of Petersburg's many trenches.

"I have never felt any sort of fondness for war and have never advocated it, except as a means of peace." Ulysses S. Grant

Grant at Cold Harbor, where he lost more than 12,000 men in a failed attack on Lee's army.

WILLIAM T. SHERMAN

Sherman's plan in invading Georgia was to cause as much damage as possible, breaking the Southerners' will to continue the war. His army destroyed everything in its path and lived by seizing supplies from the civilian population.

BURNING ATLANTA

Sherman led his army to Atlanta, the capital of Georgia, which he captured on September 2, 1864. He ordered all the people living there to leave the city, which he then burned. In the South, such brutal actions made Sherman the most hated Union general.

Sherman's men destroying railroad tracks in Atlanta.

MARCHING TO THE SEA

After leaving Atlanta, Sherman headed southeast to the sea. As he advanced, thousands of slaves fled their plantations to join him. Sherman welcomed them. The federal government heard nothing from Sherman until December, when he sent a **telegram** to Lincoln saying: "I beg to present you as a Christmas gift the city of Savannah." He then marched his army north into South Carolina, planning to link up with Grant's army in Virginia.

Sherman's army entering the Confederate city of Savannah on the coast of Georgia.

SURRENDER

In April 1865, Robert E. Lee's army, with its supply routes cut off and heavily outnumbered by Grant's army, could no longer defend Petersburg, Virginia.

Lee abandoned Petersburg and retreated west, pursued by the Union army. He reached Appomattox, where trains awaited with supplies, but Grant had got there first. The Confederates were surrounded and outnumbered by five to one. Lee realized that he had no choice but to surrender.

Lee's defeated Confederate army lay down their weapons.

LEE MEETS GRANT

On April 9, the two generals met in the house of a merchant named Wilmer McLean to discuss the surrender. Lee wore a smart new uniform with a sash, while Grant wore muddy pants and an ordinary soldier's jacket. Grant had a great respect for Lee and later wrote, "I felt like anything rather than rejoicing at the downfall of a foe who had fought so long and valiantly."

Grant (left) shaking hands with his greatest opponent, Robert E. Lee (right).

SURRENDER TERMS

Under Grant's terms of surrender, Lee's officers had to sign paroles: promises made on behalf of their men that they would no longer fight the government. The Union victors gave food to the hungry Confederates and then let them go home. Grant allowed the Southern soldiers to keep their horses, which they would need when they returned to their farms.

SURRENDER OF GEN. LEE!

A celebration of the Union victory, printed in Detroit on the day after Lee's surrender.

"The Year of Jubilee has come! Let all the People Rejoice!"

200 GUNS WILL BE FIRED

On the Campus Martius,

AT 3 O'CLOCK TO-DAY, APRIL 10,

To Celebrate the Victories of our Armies.

Every Man, Woman and Child is hereby ordered to be on hand prepared to Sing and Rejoice. The crowd are expected to join in singing Patriotic Songs.

ALL PLACES OF BUSINESS MUST BE CLOSED AT 2 O'CLOCK.

Hurrah for Grant and his noble Army.

By Order of the People.

"The war is over. The rebels are our countrymen again."

Ulysses S. Grant to his men at Appomattox.

LEE'S FAREWELL

Following his surrender, Lee wrote a farewell address to his men. He thanked them and told them that they had been forced to "yield to overwhelming numbers and resources." After the war, Lee worked to heal the divisions between North and South. He said, "I am rejoiced that slavery is abolished. I believe it will be greatly for the interests of the South."

er the war, illustrated copies of Lee's farewell dress decorated many Southern homes.

JEFFERSON DAVIS IS IMPRISONED

Meanwhile, the Confederate President, Jefferson Davis, had fled Richmond, hoping to reach Texas and continue the war. But he was captured in Georgia and imprisoned in Fort Monroe for two years. Unlike Lee, Davis was hated in the North.

THE ASSASSINATION OF LINCOLN

On April 14, 1865, just five days after the Confederates' surrender, Abraham Lincoln was shot while watching a play in a Washington theater. His killer was an actor named John Wilkes Booth.

Three days before his **assassination**, President Lincoln had made a speech in front of a big crowd in Washington. He talked of his plans to heal the divisions between the North and South and mentioned the possibility of giving freed slaves the vote. The crowd, celebrating the Union victory, cheered wildly. But one listener, John Wilkes Booth, told a friend, "This is the last speech he will ever make."

A ticket to Ford's Theatre, wh[...]
Booth had previously acted a[...]
where he shot Lincoln.

Lincoln speaks of reuniting America on the steps of the White House, the President's residence and workplace.

JOHN WILKES BOOTH

John Wilkes Booth was a famous actor who had spent the war years appearing in Northern theaters. A strong supporter of slavery and the Confederacy, Booth felt guilty that he had not fought for the South. He hated President Lincoln, whom he blamed for starting the war.

PLOTS

Booth had been plotting against Lincoln since 1864. With a group of fellow conspirators, he planned to kidnap Lincoln and then exchange him for Confederate prisoners. Nothing came of this and once the war was lost, there was no point in kidnapping the President. For this reason, Booth decided to assassinate him instead.

Ford's Theatre, Washington, where the assassination took place on Good Friday 1865.

THE ASSASSIN STRIKES

n the evening of April 14, 1865,
ncoln went to watch a comedy play
lled *Our American Cousin* at Ford's
heatre. He was seated with his wife
d two friends in a box overlooking
e stage. At about 10.45 p.m., Booth
ept into the box and shot Lincoln at
ose range in the back of the head. The
esident died the next morning.

This painting shows
the assassination and
the shocked reaction of
Lincoln's wife and friends.

War Department, Washington, April 20. 1865.

$100,000 REWARD!

THE MURDERER

Of our late beloved President, ABRAHAM LINCOLN,

IS STILL AT LARGE.

$50,000 REWARD!

will be paid by this Department for his apprehension, in addition to any reward offered
by Municipal Authorities or State Executives.

$25,000 REWARD!

will be paid for the apprehension of JOHN H. SURRATT, one of Booth's accomplices.

$25,000 REWARD!

will be paid for the apprehension of DANIEL C. HARROLD, another of Booth's accomplices.

LIBERAL REWARDS will be paid for any information that shall conduce to the arrest of either
of the above-named criminals, or their accomplices.

All persons harboring or secreting the said persons, or either of them, or aiding or assisting their
concealment or escape, will be treated as accomplices in the murder of the President and the attempted
assassination of the Secretary of State, and shall be subject to trial before a Military Commission and
the punishment of DEATH.

Let the stain of innocent blood be removed from the land by the arrest and punishment of the
murderers.

All good citizens are exhorted to aid public justice on this occasion. Every man should consider
his own conscience charged with this solemn duty, and rest neither night nor day until it be accomplished.

EDWIN M. STANTON, *Secretary of War.*

DESCRIPTIONS—BOOTH is 5 feet 7 or 8 inches high, slender build, high forehead, black hair, black eyes, and wears a heavy black mustache.
JOHN H. SURRATT is about 5 feet 9 inches. Hair rather thin and dark; eyes rather light; no beard. Would weigh 145 or 150 pounds. Complexion rather pale
and clear, with color in his cheeks. Wore light clothes of fine quality. Shoulders square; cheek bones rather prominent; chin narrow; ears projecting at top;
head rather low and square, but broad. Parts his hair on the right side; neck rather long. His lips are firmly set. A slim man.
DANIEL C. HARROLD is 22 years of age, ... of 5 inches high, rather short... complexion, ...
eyes, weight about 140 ...

BOOTH'S ESCAPE

Booth leaped out of the box
onto the stage, injuring his leg
as he landed. After shouting
"Sic semper tyrannis!" (Thus
always to tyrants) and "The
South is avenged!" he hobbled
away, making his escape on
a horse he had left outside.
Twelve days later, Booth was
found hiding in a barn by
Union cavalrymen and was
killed in a shoot-out.

The small Derringer pistol
Booth used to kill Lincoln
was just six inches long.

As news of Lincoln's death spread,
there was a national outpouring of
grief and rewards were offered for
Booth's capture.

AFTER THE WAR

The Union victory led to a stronger federal government and gave Americans a new sense that they were citizens of a single nation.

After the surrender of the Confederacy, there was a period of **reconstruction**, which meant bringing the Southern states back into the Union. New laws gave equal legal rights to blacks. Despite these laws, white Southerners found ways to keep their superior status. Although the Civil War had freed the slaves, it would be a century before black Americans gained truly equal rights with whites.

The Lincoln Memorial in Washington, D.C. honors the President for saving the Union and freeing the slaves.

★★★★

SHARECROPPING

The freed slaves needed land. Landowners introduced a system called **sharecropping**, in which they let farmers use land in exchange for a share of their crop. Farmers also had to borrow money from the landowners to buy everything they needed to live.

Like slaves, sharecroppers were still tied to the land and to a particular landowner.

THE KU KLUX KLAN

In 1865, Confederate veterans formed a secret organization called the Ku Klux Klan. Their aim was to maintain white supremacy, using terror to keep blacks from voting. Klan members carried burning crosses and hid their identities beneath white robes that made them look terrifying.

This 1874 cartoon shows how blacks were terrorized by the Klan and other white groups.

In new screen splendor...
The most magnificent picture ever!

DAVID O. SELZNICK'S PRODUCTION OF MARGARET MITCHELL'S

"GONE WITH THE WIND"

THE LOST CAUSE

Southerners coped with defeat by creating a myth called the "Lost Cause." They imagined the prewar South as a land of kind masters and happy slaves. They claimed that the war had been lost because the Northerners fought unfairly, having had more men and war supplies. The best-known story of the "Lost Cause" is the 1936 novel *Gone with the Wind* and the 1939 film version of it.

LINCOLN'S LEGACY

Abraham Lincoln's Gettysburg Address has continued to inspire Americans with the ideal of what the U.S. can be. On the steps of the Lincoln Memorial in 1963, the great campaigner for civil rights, Martin Luther King, Jr., gave his famous "I have a dream" speech. He began with words that echoed the Gettysburg Address.

"Five-score years ago, a great American, in whose symbolic shadow we stand today, signed the Emancipation Proclamation. This momentous decree came as a great beacon light of hope to millions of Negro slaves."

Martin Luther King, Jr.

GLOSSARY

ABOLITIONISTS
People who campaign to abolish something, such as slavery.

AMPUTATION
To cut off part of someone's body, especially a wounded or diseased limb.

ARMORY
A storehouse for weapons.

ARTILLERY
Large weapons, such as cannon, operated by crews of men.

ASSASSINATION
The planned killing of an important person, usually for political reasons.

BLOCKADE
Cutting off a country (or port) from the outside world. Blockades use ships to stop goods or people entering or leaving.

CAMPAIGN
A series of military operations, linked together with a common aim.

CANDIDATE
A person seeking public office, such as that of President.

CASUALTIES
Military term for soldiers lost to an army following a battle. It includes those killed, wounded, captured, and missing.

CONFEDERACY
A group of states; in particular, the name of the union of 11 Southern states that seceded from the U.S. in 1861.

CONSCRIPTION
Forced service in an army.

COTTON GIN
A machine to separate cotton fibers from the seeds, ready to make into cloth.

DEMOCRATS
The Democratic Party is the oldest political party in the United States and supported slavery before the Civil War.

DRILL
The process of training soldiers in military procedures, such as firing weapons, by making them perform the actions repeatedly.

EMANCIPATION
Being set free from something.

FEDERAL
To do with a group of states that have united under a central government called a federal government.

FLAGSHIP
Ship of the commander of a fleet. It is called a flagship because it carries the flag of the commander.

FORAGING
Searching for supplies of food and other items such as firewood.

HAVERSACK
A bag carried by a strap over one shoulder.

IRONCLAD
A nineteenth-century warship covered with iron plates for protection.

KNAPSACK
A bag with two shoulder straps, carried on the back.

LEGISLATURE
A law-making assembly.

MASS-PRODUCE
To make something in large amounts, often using machinery.

PICKETS
Small groups of soldiers sent out to watch for enemy movements or posted around army camps to protect them from surprise attack.

PLANTATIONS

Large farming estates where crops were grown by workers who lived on the estate.

RATIONS

A fixed regular allowance of food distributed to soldiers.

REBEL

A Union slang term for Confederates, whom they described as having rebelled against the United States.

RECONSTRUCTION

The process by which the Southern states were brought back into the U.S. following the Civil War.

RIFLE

A gun, fired from shoulder level, with a spiral groove inside its barrel. The groove, which makes the bullet spin when fired, increases the rifle's range and accuracy.

SECEDE

To formally withdraw from the membership of a body, such as a federation of states.

SHARECROPPING

A system in which landowners allowed farmers to use land to grow crops in exchange for a share of the crop.

SIEGE

A military operation in which an army surrounds a town or fortified place, in order to capture it.

SLAVES

Human beings treated as property and made to work without pay by slave owners.

TELEGRAPH

A device to send messages long distances, using electrical signals passed along wires.

TELEGRAM

A short message sent by telegraph.

TORPEDOES

In the nineteenth century, torpedoes were floating mines used to blow up enemy ships. Today, torpedoes are underwater self-propelled missiles.

UNDERGROUND RAILROAD

Name for the secret routes used by American abolitionists to help slaves escape to freedom.

UNION

A group of states joined together to form one country. The name refers to the Northern states in the Civil War.

VOLUNTEER

Someone who willingly joins up to serve in an army.

WHIP

A slang term for "to defeat."

Sandy Creek
NEW YORK

An Imprint of Sterling Publishing
387 Park Avenue South
New York, NY 10016

SANDY CREEK and the distinctive Sandy Creek logo are registered trademarks of Barnes & Noble, Inc.

Text © 2013 by Carlton Books

Illustrations © 2013 by Carlton Books

This 2013 edition published by Sandy Creek.

Senior Editor: Paul Virr
Senior Art Editor: Jake da'Costa
Illustrations: Peter Liddiard
Picture Research: Ben White
Production: Dawn Cameron
Consultant: Richard Campbell

ISBN 978-1-4351-4944-1

Manufactured in Dongguan, China

Lot# 2 4 6 8 10 9 7 5 3 1

06/13

INDEX

PHOTO CREDITS

The publishers would like to thank the following sources for their kind permission to reproduce the pictures in this book.

Key, T=top, L=left, R=right, B=bottom

Alamy: 42t

Bridgeman Art Library: /American Antiquarian Society: 16b, /© Civil War Archive: 18b, 19l, 21bl, 21b, /Gettysburg National Military Park Museum/Photo © Civil War Archive: 20b, /Museum of the Confederacy/Photo © Civil War Archive: 17l, 19l, 20l, /Collection of the New-York Historical Society: 12l, /Peter Newark American Pictures: 6bl, 30-31t, /Stapleton Collection: 32b

Corbis: /Bettmann: 33, 35, 39t

DK Images: 11bl

Getty Images: 24t, 28b, 39b, 42br, /Bridgeman Art Library: 7r, /SuperStock: 36

iStockphoto.com: 35bl

Library of Congress, Prints & Photographs Division: 1, 2-3, 4, 4b, 5t, 7l, 7br, 8-9, 10, 10-11t, 11tl, 11b, 12, 12br, 13t, 13l, 13b, 14-15, 16-17, 18l, 18t, 20t, 20br, 22-23, 24-25, 26-27, 28-29, 30-31, 32, 33tl, 33tr, 34, 37t, 37r, 38, 39tl, 40-41t, 41bl, 41br, 42bl, 42r, 43, 44, 45l

Photo 12: /Archives du 7e Art: 45t

Thinkstockphotos.co.uk: 5c, 6-7, 37b, 44

Topfoto.co.uk: 45bl, /Fotomas: 5b, /Granger Collection: 5tl, 6br, 40b, 41t

US National Archives: 2, 10, (P.G.T Beauregard)

Every effort has been made to acknowledge correctly and contact the source and/or copyright holder of each picture. Carlton Books Limited apologizes for any unintentional errors or omissions, which would be corrected in future editions of this book.